Singing
Fierce
Gratitude

*Daily Poems of
Abundance, Generosity,
and Gratitude*

TINA DATSKO DE SÁNCHEZ

Foreword by Molly Baskette

Open Waters Publishing
an imprint of The Pilgrim Press
1300 East 9th Street,
Cleveland, Ohio 44114
thepilgrimpress.com

Published 2023.

Printed on acid-free paper.

Library of Congress Cataloging-in-Publication Data on file.
LCCN: 2021943794

ISBN (paper) 978-0-8298-1233-6

Printed in The United States of America.

Original cover artwork by Loryn Spangler-Jones
Book and cover design by Meredith Pangrace

For my high school English teachers,
Miss Reynolds and Dr. Swenson-Davis,
who taught me to think and write—
when writing saved my life.

CONTENTS

20. Abundance meets the eyes

21. Life is in the now—

22. The Beloved is here, now, in this moment.

23. Mine the gold that is within you.

24. God gives you an abundance of opportunities

25. Let the sun teach us about abundance;

26. Truly, there is nothing but abundance—

27. Jacarandas put forth their blossoms,

28. In fluid muscles and supple spine,

29. All is provided in just the right measure.

30. Experience abundance in sunlight flashing from day lilies.

Thirty Poems of Generosity

1. When all is given to us,

2. Does not the sun caress us each with golden rays?

3. The olive tree reaches out new tendrils

4. In the morning, give to the body stretching

5. The sun warms the crown of my head;

6. Does not the Beloved give us sunlight?

7. Asleep, we are like fleas gorged with blood,

8. The secret to generosity is being open.

9. You have been made for generosity.

10. God's generosity knows no bounds.

11. On Saturday, planting a bowl of succulents,

12. The Friend has given me so many friends:

13. The tree of life bears many fruits:

14. Let the love in my heart pour into yours,

15. Friends, the Beloved has given us all we need:

16. This fullness I feel, this welling up of love,

17. God's generosity is so complete.

18. How can we be so blindered not to perceive

19. This light giving birth to the universe

20. Giving away to all the merit of your practice,

21. The hibiscus bud does not hold back;

22. Watching wind rattle the palm fronds

23. Beloved, open my eyes to your generosity.

24. In a dream, she shows me the folly

25. There is a fullness in life—

26. Why do we need to keep remembering God?

27. Wherever you are, God is with you.

28. Friends, remember God's generosity is boundless.

29. Friends, these boxes, these rooms

30. Stretching our limbs in yoga

Thirty Poems of Gratitude

1. Gratitude is the frosting on the cake.

2. Sunflowers open their hearts with gratitude;

3. Breath rushes into the body

4. Gratitude is the key to the future.

5. Gratitude for the journey

6. Gratitude for today, for the miracle

7. Gratitude for sunlight shining on the lemon tree

8. Hiking in shimmering mountain air,

9. My husband turns the pineapples upside down

10. Above its burnished leaves, the heavenly bamboo

11. Under soft gray skies, a quiet day of remembrance:

12. Gratitude is a choice.

13. Isn't gratitude the natural song of all things?

14. When we finally grasp that all is unfolding

15. On a day when two friends celebrate their wedding,

16. How miraculous that where the sun touches

17. The way the sun and rain and earth

18. Gratitude for the unfolding of life:

19. Can we be grateful even for change?

20. Even this pain today—a rib out of place—

21. Beloved, in morning stillness you are here.

22. When we pause and breathe,

23. When the Tibetan singing bowl rings,

24. What if we are meant to be plugged in?

25. What if God is

26. What am I grateful for right now?

27. Another skill to learn along the path

Acknowledgments

FOREWORD

I am sitting at a rough-hewn picnic table in a group campground high above the bustle of the Bay Area, at my community's all church retreat.

I am the first one awake. A plane flies overhead, as oblivious of me as the hawk in search of breakfast one canyon over. Far below me, the world continues: train whistles, Saturday traffic, and the inaudible misery and joy of millions of people living precariously at this hinge of history. That misery and joy, anxiety and anger, all the epic feelings spawned by modernity and its discontents is right now bumping up against my more immediate reality: a ukulele left out, the embers of last night's campfire ready to be stoked to a breakfast blaze again, all the detritus of music, laughter and communion. Gratitude consumes me, in spite of all that is blooming below me. In this moment, we are living through plague, climate chaos, extreme economic inequality, racial terrorism, and Christian nationalism. But "ours is not a caravan of despair," as Rumi once wrote, sweet honey which is itself a medicine.

Rumi would know. He was born in what is now Afghanistan and fled violence on a long journey that took him through Iran, Iraq, Syria and finally Turkey. He didn't wait to start giving thanks until all was well. He lived on the edges, and on the edge—and from that edge invited us consistently into the playful divine, the sense that joy was not a someday-when-this-is-all-better proposition but a right-here-right-now way of experiencing the world.

Into our current topsy-turvy, whirling dervish of a world, Tina Datsko de Sánchez offers a miracle: the resurrection of Rumi and Hafiz's voices. Her series of spare, playful poems draw on images from the natural world and our universal human longings. She has given us a doorway—90 doorways, to be exact—into another reality, without leaving our own. We can step over the threshold and reveal the ordinary as extraordinary, right where we are, without delay.

In this time that is so fraught, to take sabbath may feel like a guilty pleasure, and sometimes more guilt than pleasure. But it is not. Sabbath is a commandment from God, made so for the very reason that God knew what was coming and that we would need to find rest, joy, and attend to the holy as our sacred duty.

Whether you imbibe these poems as a one-a-day spiritual succor, or a big bingeworthy draught of divinity, they will set your feet sunward. Even now, abundance, generosity and gratitude are the gift and the gauntlet we have been thrown from God. All we have to do is enter in to that which awaits.

Christlove,
Molly Baskette

PREFACE

I began writing the poems for *Singing Fierce Gratitude* in March of 2013, again as part of a spiritual practice during Lent. Writing the poems three or four days a week was a way to intensify my listening for spiritual guidance. The first series, "Thirty Poems of Abundance," helped me to train my antennae on that theme. How true it is that whatever we focus on seems to appear more readily. I began to see through the lens of abundance and notice it more in my surroundings—in trees, sunlight, blades of grass, moments with friends and family. And that profusion came across as a sign of the outpouring of love from the heart of the universe.

This energy flowed on and shifted to writing "Thirty Poems of Generosity," starting in May of 2013. While in the outer world my spouse and I continued dealing with health challenges, my poetry time gave me a healing space of connection with the Divine. In the poems, generosity appeared as the natural response to abundance; that as we breathe in abundance, we breathe out generosity. Generosity was an essential part of keeping the flow going—pumping love from the heart of the universe and giving it away to make space for more.

In January of 2014, I began the "Thirty Poems of Gratitude," coinciding with the release of my bilingual poetry book, *The Delirium of Simón Bolívar*. The culmination of a book that began with several grants I received in 1984 was a source of satisfaction and gratitude. As I shared the book at conferences, churches, art galleries, house parties, bookstores and universities, my gratitude deepened. I felt grateful for family and friends, for the gift of poetry and the blessing of life. Writing these poems was a vehicle for developing gratitude as a spiritual practice.

I am also struck by how gratitude can spring from an experience of what we have come through and survived. In fall 2013, in my role as Poet in Residence at the First Congregational Church of Long Beach, I decided to write a poem expressing gratitude to the church leaders who guided the congregation through a transition planning process and hiring a new Senior Minister. I asked the Associate Minister, Rev. John Forrest Douglas, to steer me to a fitting scriptural passage as a jumping-off point. He suggested I consider Miriam's song after the Israelite's safe passage through the Red Sea. This is the poem that showed up:

STANDING IN GRATITUDE, LIVING IN JOY

Standing in gratitude, living in joy,
we reach beyond old wounds and pain.

The waters have parted,
and we have crossed over to new life,
leaving our fears on the distant shore.

Standing in gratitude, living in joy,
we move forward into abundant new life.

God has parted the seas of fear and doubt.
Let us raise tambourines to dance and shout,
giving thanks to our God.

Standing in gratitude, living in joy,
we build a community of trust and love.

God is with us in our falling and rising,
in our living and dying,
in our growing and healing this world.

Standing in gratitude, living in joy,
we dance and sing our praise to God!

I am delighted to be able to share with readers this four-book series of interfaith spiritual poetry. Folks to whom I mentioned the process of finding publication have suggested I tell the story. It was something of a moonshot—a perfect conjunction of elements brought together, I believe, by divine guidance.

While I continued writing these short poems, I also began to consider ways of sharing them. Since they were conceived through practicing William Stafford's advice to "Lower your standards," they were written without literary ambition, a departure from previous work I had written for literary competitions and magazines. I sensed a different approach would be needed for finding a publisher in this new-to-me landscape.

I began moving forward by listening to intuition and trusting its guidance. I was led to three women, whose wisdom and generosity made this publication possible. When the Reverend Mary Scifres came to FCCLB as a consultant, because of her background editing *The Abington Worship Annual*, my intuition suggested to ask her advice. She was immensely helpful. After reading *Swimming in God*, she recommended I approach The Pilgrim Press and ask FCCLB's Senior Minister, the Reverend Elena Larssen, to write a letter of introduction. Pastor Elena said she would be happy to write the letter and also call her colleague, the Reverend Rachel Hackenberg, who had recently joined the press as Managing Editor. I sent the proposal for the book series to Reverend Hackenberg, and it was subsequently accepted for publication.

What amazed me about this process was that through following the "pathless path" of intuition, I was guided to the appropriate press at the appropriate time. After twenty years of contributing poetry to FCCLB as my form of a tithe, it felt that doors were opening because generosity and cooperation create opportunity.

—Tina Datsko de Sánchez
Long Beach, California

"Wouldn't it be a blessing if we can be grateful for everything which comes our way no matter what?"
From *Reiki Insights* by Frans Stiene

Thirty Poems of Abundance

1.

There's no getting away from it.
Life is effervescent.

Look around you: the trees are waving
their branches at you, saying, life is a miracle!

What sunlight and water do for the trees,
divine love is doing for you right now.

2.

Whatever we need is there for us.
This world is a great banquet,
filled with a richness of possibility.

So even if we are too blindered to see
the piles of goodies God has laid out for us,
we can learn to use our sense of smell.

3.

Can we even wrap our minds around
the meaning of 'unlimited'?

The Beloved's love for us is unlimited.
The Beloved's delight in us is unlimited.

The joy that can pour through us is unlimited.
Can our delight in God become unlimited?

4.

We have all the gold we could ever want;
it's in the sunlight falling freely on us.

We have all the greenbacks we could ever need;
they are blades of grass and leaves of trees.

We have all the wealth we can imagine;
it's in the loving of friends, family, and the Beloved.

5.

We have been given all that we need.
We have each other.

And the love flowing between us
pumps love from the heart of the universe.

As you lean on me and I on you,
the Beloved's tender palm is cupped beneath us.

6.

Did you know the heart is infinite?
There is nothing it cannot contain.

Oceans of love are available to it.
Forests of compassion fill it.

Stars and planets are ever expanding,
when the heart is an open door to God.

7.

Be the Beloved—let your actions, thoughts, and words
form what the Beloved would do, think, say.

Erase reactions, erase ego, throw out the clutter
of negativity blocking the soul's flow.

Be the Beloved—let pure love and light
dance through every atom, erasing 'self' and 'other'.

8.

What if thankfulness nourishes God?
What if the outpouring of extravagant gratitude
fertilizes the Ground of All Being?

What if enriching the soil of the creative heart
of the Universe returns unimaginable
abundance and delight to all beings?

9.

First day of spring—the pomegranate's
new growth is budding red.
The olive tree bears pale green shoots.

Spring equinox—just the right balance
of sunlight and darkness to trigger new growth.
Where in me can balance bring forth abundance?

10.

Some days the pain of heartbreak tears us apart—
the shredding of all that felt familiar,
the collapse of all that felt reliable.

Some days the breaking apart roars like a waterfall
and sucks us down into deep pools of sorrow
where there is nothing but God.

11.
All that you need is here
in the beauty of this morning.

In the way the sunlight reveals the olive tree.
In the way the breeze lets branches breathe.

An abundance of life is right here before you—
just focus your heart and drink it in.

12.

Let the breeze caress your cheek.
Let light fall upon you and impregnate you.
The Beloved has chosen you.

There will never be a better moment than now
to carry abundant love to full term,
giving birth eternally to God.

13.

The Easter lily is heavy with blooms
and fragrant with the sweetness of life.

Earth's mothering energy nourishes growth,
with fertility spawning abundance.

The mother within is here to nurture the soul,
to kiss its brow and wipe away its tears.

14.

Life is as abundant as sunlight.
Love is as abundant as water.
Peace is as abundant as breath.

We are here to be bathed in
sunlight and water to grow and blossom,
here to be breathed into by God.

15.

Life is sweeter because the palm tree
stands tall in the sunlight.

Life is sweeter because the sparrows
flit about the yard picking up seeds.

Life is sweeter when we sense the Beloved
speaks to us and touches us through all things.

16.

Living in abundance is touching
the eternal in the everyday.

The tang of grapefruit on the tongue.
The sweet warmth of cranberry tea.

The Beloved gives us all these delights
that we may delight in the miracle of now.

17.

Abundance resides in the memory
of eating s'mores around a lakeside campfire.

Abundance resides in being fully present
to make music, dance, or love.

Abundance resides in the room of the soul
as it opens onto infinite spaciousness.

18.

Look for abundance in spaciousness
and gentleness and patience.

Look for abundance in your heart
as it opens more fully to God.

Look for abundance in your arms
as they joyously embrace a sister or brother.

19.

The Beloved has populated this earthly world
with teeming abundance—trees, flowers, fruits,
birds, fish, and all manner of beings.

Surely in the spiritual world the Beloved
showers us with equal abundance,
where the eternal is present when we are.

20.

Abundance meets the eyes
in scarlet blooming lilies.

Abundance meets the ears
in joyous birdsong greeting the dawn.

Abundance meets the heart
in gentle whispers of the Beloved:
I am here. Come dance with me.

21.

Life is in the now—
in this dawn greeting your vision,
in this birdsong cheering your ears.

Be present and rejoice—
in this breeze stirring your hair,
the Beloved is here, now, embracing you.

22.

The Beloved is here, now, in this moment.
Reach out and touch the sunlight,
its warmth streaming divine love.

Reach out and grasp a brother's hand,
embrace a sister's weary shoulders—
God will never be closer than in this moment.

23.

Mine the gold that is within you.
The Divine has built rich deposits
of precious ore within your soul.

Your alchemy of love and compassion
fills the Beloved's storerooms
with true wealth to meet the needs of all.

24.

God gives you an abundance of opportunities
to turn and be embraced.

If you miss this ferry to the Divine,
another one will be along soon.

But, friends, why not board now and sail to the party,
so as not to miss a drop of music and laughter?

25.

Let the sun teach us abundance;
she gives her light without stopping, without fearing.

Let clouds teach us abundance;
their rain that falls, comes back to them again.

Let the moon teach us abundance;
the dust of myriad stars lives on in us.

26.

Truly, there is nothing but abundance—
the universe is so large it must hide in your heart.

The power of the sun is so disarming,
it makes its home in the twinkle of your eye.

Where there is everything, there is light and shadow,
love and tenderness, in just the right measure.

27.

Jacarandas put forth their blossoms,
filling the sky with lavender fireworks.

May explodes onto the scene
with vermilion bougainvillea.

God has us surrounded.
The flowers point their barrels at us.

We may as well put our hands up, heavenward,
and surrender to abundance with gratitude.

28.

In fluid muscles and supple spine,
in glands and hormones guiding life,
in breath and heartbeats—abundance.

In the body's rhythms, the mind's ingenuity,
the heart's dreams—such lavishness.
What of the universes within your very soul?

29.

All is provided in just the right measure.
Rain falls, lavishing the earth with water
and polishing the glass of the air.

Sun light breaks through, lifting rain skyward again.
Gently held in the cycles of life,
let ecstasy embrace the perfection of now.

30.

Experience abundance in sunlight flashing from day lilies.
Savor abundance in the night breeze wafting jasmine.

Receive abundance in the raucous call of birds at dawn.
Recognize abundance in the sweet completeness of a pear.

Live abundance as love wells up in your heart
and know the Beloved is with us always.

Thirty Poems of Generosity

1.

When all is given to us,
there's nothing left to do but give back.

When we inhale sweet oxygen from plants,
we exhale back to them the carbon they need.

When we inhale pure love from God,
we exhale back caring and generosity.

2.

Does not the sun caress us each with golden rays?
Does not the rain nurse the earth at its breast?
Does not the earth deliver from its loins the ecstatic harvest?

Generosity is the way of nature.
The Beloved pours out the sweet wine,
our lives crystal decanters for filling our neighbor's glass.

3.

The olive tree reaches out new tendrils
in all directions, basking in the sun.

From pruned branches, the pomegranate tree's
new red leaves explode outward.

All that is given is received, generating
new life, then given back again.

4.

In the morning, give to the body stretching
and nourishment, give to the mind meditation.

In the evening, give to the heart friendship and caring,
give to the spirit poetry, music and dance.

The cycle of giving spins through us,
and spins us toward enlightenment.

5.

The sun warms the crown of my head;
the chair supports me so perfectly.

The breeze blows past my nostrils,
filling my lungs with life-giving air.

All that is needed, appears. The Beloved
endows our needs with boundless generosity.

6.

Does not the Beloved give us sunlight?
And from that, the plants that nourish us
and the energy coursing in our bodies?

Does not the Beloved give us radiant love?
And from that, family that supports us
and friends whose laughter helps our spirits leap?

7.

Asleep, we are like fleas gorged with blood,
as divine generosity pours into us—
breath, light, love.

As we awaken, we can become
a sponge, a vessel, a channel,
breathing out light and love to all creation.

8.

The secret to generosity is being open.
Open the floodgates so God's love
pouring through you, pours out to all.

The secret to generosity is being transparent.
Thin the veil of your mind so God's light
shining through you, shines for all.

9.

You have been made for generosity.
Be as generous as the breeze cooling you.
Be as generous as olive branches swaying.

Be as generous as the sun giving life to the Earth.
The Beloved's heart is pouring forth all existence.
Now let all existence pour through you.

10.

God's generosity knows no bounds.
Golden wheat fields are our tablecloth,
the sun and moon our dinner plates.

The starry sky our comforter,
the ocean sings us a lullaby. How can
we stand in gratitude for constant miracles?

11.

On Saturday, planting a bowl of succulents,
we take cuttings and insert them in muddy soil,
their turgid leaves jade, garnet, amethyst.

By Sunday, they are already standing tall
and growing toward the light—such radical
resilience and wisdom in translucent gems.

12.

The Friend has given me so many friends:
the olive tree that shades me,
the tomato plant that feeds me,

the honeybee that pollinates the flowers,
the clouds that bring life-giving rain,
the eyes, hands, hearts that know and give and love.

13.

The tree of life bears many fruits:
peaches, pears, grapefruit, pomegranates.

How surprised we are that some fruit
tastes bitter when we're expecting sweet.

The wise among us know the Beloved
nourishes us with each experience to meet a need.

14.

Let the love in my heart pour into yours,
and the love in your heart pour into mine.

There is an endless well of love the Friend
has dug for us into the cool depths.

All we need to do is pump it out,
which we can do with each embrace.

15.

Friends, the Beloved has given us all we need:
this breath that breathes us moment by moment.

Now let us play a game—give breath back
to the plants and they will give it back to you.

Then give breath to loved ones
in sweet speech, kisses, and song.

When we breathe into one another,
we are saving each other's lives.

16.

This fullness I feel, this welling up of love,
is divine generosity pouring through me.

The trick is to unclog the spring,
to dig down to where the Divine meets us.

Here's a shovel; I'll take the pickaxe.
Now take a deep breath and dig!

17.

God's generosity is so complete.
Does the sun ever hold back its life-giving radiance?

Does the rain hold back its nourishing waters?
Does the grain hold back its sustaining energy?

All is given to us in abundance, fulfilling
the possibility of God in us to shine on all.

18.

How can we be so blindered not to perceive
the sun pouring out its heart for us,
the ocean giving birth to our whole lives?

How can we be so stubborn not to understand
we are each other's arms and legs—
the mouths to be fed are each other's hearts?

19.

This light giving birth to the universe
opens like a flower, like a galaxy,
spins everything into being.

And the universe in my heart,
in your heart, spins just as miraculously
and spaciously its dance of being.

20.

Giving away to all the merit of your practice,
giving it all away, giving your self away,

feels like a giant sail unfurling,
whooshing open into immensity where nothing

small remains, where Spirit is the sail
and Love is the wind carrying it skyward.

21.

The hibiscus bud does not hold back;
it unfurls completely, sings its radiant song
for its entire day of life.

Give yourself fully; unfurl the blossom
of your soul, dance your shining dance
for this entire day we call a lifetime.

22.

Watching wind rattle the palm fronds
and clouds scud across the sky—
alternating shadow, sun, shadow, sun.

This planet, this entire universe, is in flux,
yet gravity keeps us from falling off;
gravity holds us in place.

Find that force that anchors you
to dance in the palm of God's hand.

23.

Beloved, open my heart to your generosity.
Its sight is thickly veiled
to the treasures you set before me each day.

Draw back these veils of expectations and assumptions.
Let me sense what is truly there—
every breath a treasure, every soul a friend.

24.

In a dream, she shows me the folly
of thinking my project funded only by money.

Open your heart to see the many hands
that donated skills and gifts.

Open your soul to allow the flow
of possibility, generosity, abundance.

25.

There is a fullness in life—
a perfection in each moment just as it is.

The bird on the branch knows it and sings.
The lemon tree knows it and bears fruit.

There is absolutely nothing we need to do,
only sit in stillness and bask in the glow of the now.

26.

Why do we need to keep remembering God?
Because at night it's easy to believe the sun is gone,
when it's just doing its job of spreading light everywhere.

Why do we need to keep remembering God?
To recognize the Beloved is always here,
giving us all we need and ready, so ready, to help.

27.

Wherever you are, God is with you.
However you are, God is with you.

It is only our own hands, held up to our eyes
playing peek-a-boo, that hide God from sight.

It is only unkindness to ourselves and others
that blinders us to God's outpouring grace.

28.

Friends, remember God's generosity is boundless.
Is there any day the sun stopped halfway
in its course and walked home?

Is there any night the moon
didn't feel like dancing for us?
God's flow is constant and unending,
God's arms always ready to embrace.

29.

Friends, these boxes, these rooms
we live in are not our lives.

These thoughts we are accustomed to
can become a cage, and we the caged lion.

Let us rattle the bars of our cages,
startling us each awake to discover
the cage door was never, ever locked.

30.

Stretching our limbs in yoga
creates a spaciousness within.

It is like a virgin sail,
new and bright this day—

waiting to fill and billow with inspiration
as God breathes generosity into our souls.

Thirty Poems of Gratitude

1.

Gratitude is the frosting on the cake.
When we can sense the perfection of life just as it is,
perceive the perfection of all beings—

every planet, animal, person—
then the leavening of love raises us like cake,
and gratitude spreads sweetness from edge to edge.

2.

Sunflowers open their hearts with gratitude;
golden petals reflect back sun giving life.

Palm trees raise branches in gratitude,
swaying with ecstasy in the Divine's breath.

All creation beckons us to learn its secret:
dissolve in gratitude, becoming one with God.

3.

Breath rushes into the body
like a thousand joyous children to their playground.

Each cell jumps up and down with glee;
each electron pirouettes in ecstasy.

Can there be any sane response to this
raucous combustion called life other than gratitude?

4.

Gratitude is the key to the future.
Sending forward gratitude to all beings
builds a bridge from this now to that now.

Gratitude opens a door in the heart
to a place of spaciousness, a ballroom
where the Friend, and all friends, dance.

5.

Gratitude for the journey
and for the traveling companions.

Gratitude for this mountain path
revealing, at each turn, new vistas.

Gratitude for the climb: concentration,
quickened heartbeat, a friend's hand
to steady you through the rough spots.

6.

Gratitude for today, for the miracle
of sunlight warming skin,
for breath opening ribs like a bellows.

Gratitude for a step to take,
a path to walk, a hill to climb
with friends to view the truth.

7.

Gratitude for sunlight shining on the lemon tree
and ripening the lemons' offering.

The night's storming has passed;
a gentle breeze stirs the palm fronds.

Gratitude, Beloved, for this moment right now,
for its perfection and abundance.

8.

Hiking in shimmering mountain air,
sitting circled around a campfire's warmth,
we sense our connection to God and each other.

In bright lines of poetry, in laughter and song,
the truth of our being emerges: each wild, precious life
is joined with all, immersed in God.

9.

My husband turns the pineapples upside down
and stands them on their sturdy leaves
to let their sweetness follow gravity and fill them completely.

Could it be that God turns us upside down
and stands us on our stubborn thoughts
to let our sweetness follow gravity and fill us completely?

10.

Above its burnished leaves, the heavenly bamboo
puts forth clusters of blood-red berries,
last season's blossoms come to fruition.

Side by side, on a new stalk, white buds
explode into golden star blossoms—
the fulfilled flowing into the possible.

11.

Under soft gray skies, a quiet day of remembrance:
Guitar chords strum as if caressing nerves
into relaxation. Loved ones who've left

this world seem to hover near
in a mist of love. Gratitude opens my heart
to drink in this all-ness of God.

12.

Gratitude is a choice.
We can view the sky as half-empty
or half-full of sunshine.

We can view the day as half-empty
or half-full of blessings.
Choosing gratitude welcomes joy.

13.

Isn't gratitude the natural song of all things?
Isn't the sunlight singing in gratitude for its radiance?
Isn't the wind singing in gratitude for its freedom?

Aren't the flowers singing in gratitude for this very moment?
The moon and I are singing in gratitude
for the magnificent gift of reflecting the Divine.

14.

When we finally grasp that all is unfolding
mysteriously toward the greater good of all beings,
then our hearts unfurl like rosebuds opening.

When we finally trust that the Divine
is present in all beings and happenings,
then our souls blaze like the sun rising.

15.

On a day when two friends celebrate their wedding,
one friend's time on earth ends, and another is baptized.
What could the Beloved be showing us?

Perhaps that sorrow and joy live side by side,
like two rivers flowing together, blending their currents,
finally pouring into the ocean of all that is.

16.

How miraculous that where the sun touches
the budding roses, they turn
from pale cream to passionate crimson.

Could it be that where the Divine touches
our budding hearts, they turn
from pale intellect to compassion?

17.

The way the sun and rain and earth
collaborate to make trees grow,

just so divine love and sorrow and community
collaborate to make souls grow.

When our roots are planted firmly in connection,
our branches blossom and bear fruit.

18.

Gratitude for the unfolding of life:
the wisdom of jacaranda branches,
touched by the sun, birthing lavender blossoms.

The wisdom of oak leaves, dropping in fall
to enrich the soil and strengthen growth,
as acorns satellite outward to new lives.

19.

Can we be grateful even for change?
Even when the solidity of life cracks like thin ice,
and we fall through into uncertainty?

What if change is the music our lives dance to?
Without change, can there be music?
Without movement, can there be dance?

20.

Even this pain today—a rib out of place—
is part of the beauty of being alive.

God, breathe into me your balm of gratitude
and help me savor each moment as it unfolds.

Life stirs in my heart and spirit,
reminding me I am always in your embrace.

21.

Beloved, in morning stillness you are here.
Precious clouds diffuse the sun,
making soft and gentle your brilliance.

Jade green palm fronds ripple beckoning fingers.
A world of peace and joy awaits the attentive,
all whose hearts well sweetly with gratitude.

22.

When we pause and breathe,
when we look around and get our bearings,
we can begin to see the truth of our existence.

All is unfolding in God's time.
All is unfolding with God's help.
And we are exactly where we need to be.

23.

When the Tibetan singing bowl rings,
I feel vibration in my bones, vibration in my ears.
Where is the sound? Inside of me or outside?

Or is there no inside and no outside?
Is the sound the proof that all atoms
are as one and vibrate together?

24.

What if we are meant to be plugged in?
What if we are each cells in one cosmic body?

How miraculous to live as a sea creature,
swimming all day in divine love!

Even the stones absorb divine energy each day,
giving it back each night, keeping us warm.

25.

What if God is
a verb, an action, an attitude,
a heart overflowing with gratefulness?

What if God is
what happens when we love one another
and take care of each other?

26.

What am I grateful for right now?
Sunlight giving life to palm fronds?
Eyes, nerves, mind enabling me to see it?

Heart bursting with joy at this abundance?
Spirit at rest in connection with God and all beings?
Make your own list or feel free to borrow mine.

27.

Another skill to learn along the path
is gratitude for the challenges we encounter.

The pain of feeling unheard
is an opportunity to listen.

The pain of feeling misunderstood
is an opportunity to understand.

28.

When we release attachments,
like scabs covering old wounds,
the healed skin can emerge.

Delicate at first, like a fledgling,
our true self learns to soar,
with divine grace lifting its wings.

29.

In difficult moments, God's hand is upon me,
in the sun warming my skin.

God's breath breathes into me,
in the breeze stirring palm fronds.

God's heart wells love throughout the universe,
and my heart becomes a bubbling spring.

30.

Beloved, how can I ever thank you
for the miracle of creation,

for love beating in my heart,
for the warm embrace of loved ones?

Is there any greater thanks I can give
than joining this art of creation?

ACKNOWLEDGMENTS

Let me begin at the beginning. I am only writing today by the grace of God. My parents, Joseph and Doris Datsko, gave their five children an upbringing enriched by the arts: music and dance lessons, arts and crafts, concerts, singing in church choir. In high school, my English teachers, Miss Reynolds and Dr. Swenson-Davis, challenged me to develop my writing. In college, I majored in creative writing, choreography, and psychology of creativity through the mentoring of Professors Walter Clark, Vera Embree, and Rudolf Arnheim. My Aunt Clara also encouraged me to embrace being a writer. And when I met my soulmate, Dr. José Sánchez-H., he became the greatest champion and co-conspirator of my creative endeavors. His are the first eyes to see each poem I write, and he patiently proofreads my work before it goes out into the world.

For the growth of my writing in the direction of spiritual poetry, I want to thank some of the gardeners whose care helped it flourish. The Reverend Mary Ellen Kilsby and the Reverend Libby Tigner celebrated my early attempts. The Reverend Jerald Stinson helped me to engage collaboratively with clergy. Cathy Chambers brainstormed with me on making an artist book, a project from which all of this poetry has flowed. Later, as Moderator at the First Congregational Church of Long Beach, Cathy was instrumental in my being awarded the Aaron and Maycie Herrington Pathfinder Award and being given the honorary title of Poet in Residence, both of which opened this "pathless path" before me.

The community of the First Congregational Church of Long Beach provided fertile ground in which my creative process grew deep roots. Thus rooted, poetry began to flow through me, both for liturgical use and for these volumes. The Sacred Practices meditation group, which I co-lead with Dr. Bob Kalayjian, has offered the cross-pollination of both hearing and sharing poems. I am grateful to Dr. Bob and all my fellow meditators. Gratitude also flows to others who have been part of the FCCLB community. Megan Monaghan shared with me a collection of poetry by Hafiz that scattered more seeds. Composer Stan DeWitt set seven of the poems as "Seven Songs of Longing." Additionally, Director of Music Curtis Heard set some of the poems for liturgical use. The Reverend John Forrest Douglas made a video of one of my poems.

I especially want to thank the godmothers and godfathers of these books. The Reverend Mary Scifres read *Swimming in God* and recommended I try The Pilgrim Press. The Reverend Elena Larssen spoke with and wrote a letter of introduction for me to The Pilgrim Press, as well as the foreword to *Dancing Through Fire*. The Reverend Molly Baskette wrote an endorsement for me to send to the publisher and also the foreword for *Singing Fierce Gratitude*. The Reverend Jim Burklo gave me many doses of encouragement and wrote the foreword for *Drinking Pure Light*. The Reverend Maren Tirabassi invited me to share my poetry on her blog and wrote the foreword for *Swimming in God*.

As publisher of The Pilgrim Press, the Reverend Rachel Hackenberg humbled me with her radical welcome of the four manuscripts. I am deeply grateful to her for believing in this poetry.

Licensing coordinator Kathryn Martin has valiantly answered my many questions and helped me through the process. Program assistant Georgetta Thomas coordinated schedules and communications. Production coordinator Adam Bresnahan guided the manuscripts into book form. My gratitude to each of them as well.

My heartfelt thanks to my attorney Phillip Rosen for his thoughtful and generous support with the publishing agreements. Gratitude also to my friend Nancy Schraeder for her many years of encouragement and her careful proofreading. Many thanks as well to Suzanne Lyons, whose career coaching gave me the tools to implement my dreams.

ABOUT THE AUTHOR

Tina Datsko de Sánchez is an author and filmmaker whose work won fourteen Hopwood Awards and the Los Angeles Arts Council Award. Her writing appeared in magazines and books in several countries, including *Michigan Magazine, Nimrod, Psychological Perspectives, Sojourners* and *The Heroine's Journey Workbook.* Her bilingual poetry book, *The Delirium of Simón Bolívar,* published jointly by Floricanto Press and Berkeley Press with a foreword by Edward James Olmos, won the Phi Kappa Phi Award and a Michigan Council for the Arts Grant. She wrote and produced the feature documentary *Searching for Simón Bolívar: One Poet's Journey,* which premiered at the 30th Festival of Latin American Cinema in Trieste, Italy. Her poetry films aired on Sundance Channel and CNN Showbiz Today. She taught creative writing at The University of Michigan and screenwriting at California State University, Long Beach. She serves as Poet in Residence at the First Congregational Church in Long Beach, where she resides.

WORKS BY TINA DATSKO DE SÁNCHEZ

POETRY

Drinking Pure Light
Dancing through Fire
Swimming in God
The Delirium of Simón Bolívar (translated by José Sánchez-H.)

FILMS (as Writer/Producer)

Searching for Simón Bolívar: One Poet's Journey
The Candle
Crossing the Andes
Robinson
Domitila Speaks to the Earth
The Pomegranate
The Millstone
My General
The Man of Laws
The Delirium
News for Manuela
The Road to the Coast
Rudolf Arnheim: A Life in Art
La Paz (co-written with José Sánchez-H.)
Yo no entiendo a la gente grande

PLAYS

Manuelita
La Paz (co-authored with José Sánchez-H.)